CW00735506

NORFOLK IN WINTER

CHRIS HERRING

HALSGROVE

First published in Great Britain in 2010

Copyright © Chris Herring 2010

All rights reserved. No part of this publication may be reproduced,
stored in a retrieval system, or transmitted in any form or by any
means without the prior permission of the copyright holder.

British Library Cataloguing-in-Publication Data
A CIP record for this title is available from the British Library

ISBN 978 0 85704 055 8

HALSGROVE
Halsgrove House,
Ryelands Industrial Estate,
Bagley Road, Wellington, Somerset TA21 9PZ
Tel: 01823 653777   Fax: 01823 216796
email: sales@halsgrove.com

Part of the Halsgrove group of companies
Information on all Halsgrove titles is available at: www.halsgrove.com

Printed and bound by Grafiche Flaminia, Italy

Introduction

WINTER IS MY FAVOURITE TIME of the year for photography. I always feel there is something magical and surreal about photographing the winter landscape. Mist, fog, frost and snow can easily transform the ordinary into the extraordinary and no two mornings are ever the same. For me winter in Norfolk is not just about frosty mornings and fresh snowfall, it's also about golden reeds on the Norfolk Broads, deserted beaches, clear bright sunrises and amazing sunsets.

The varied landscape of Norfolk is a delight to photograph at all times of the year, however the winter is an especially great time to witness the unique and varied landscapes that Norfolk has to offer. It is easy to wax lyrical about our winter weather, painting an imaginary picture of glorious frosty mornings, fresh snowfall and wonderful blue skies, although in truth the average winter day in Norfolk is often dull and relatively mild compared to other areas of the UK. I think because of this, when we do have a cold snap over the region, it is quite special and the results are always striking.

The Norfolk coast is particularly beautiful in the winter months. Long gone are the summer tourists, the beaches are empty and peaceful with pristine sands bordering the tideline. Of all the areas of Norfolk, though, I feel it is the Broads which perhaps go through the greatest transformation in winter. By late summer the green reeds start to change colour and by December they have turned into a fabulous golden host. The summer cruisers are packed up in boat sheds for the winter months and all is eerily quiet along the rivers and waterways that make up the Norfolk Broads.

No two Norfolk winters are ever the same. Sometimes the season can be particularly mild, while at others times bleak and harsh with endless frosty mornings and heavy snowfalls. I must admit to being fortunate that whilst gathering images for this book we experienced one of the coldest winters for years, with unusually high amounts of snowfall and plenty of winter hoar frosts when the freezing fog deposited tiny ice crystals on every surface.

Chasing the light across the Norfolk landscape over the winter months can be a frustrating but rewarding experience. Huddled in the sand dunes and waiting for the right light whilst at the same time trying to shelter from freezing winds coming in from the North Sea is never a fun experience. But when the light does finally break through, revealing the fantastic colours of the low winter sun, it all seems worthwhile. In *Norfolk in Winter* I have tried to portray a range of winter conditions captured at different times of the day and at different times of the season. I hope these pictures help convey the best of this startling and beautiful season.

Chris Herring
2010

Overleaf: An bitterly cold winter afternoon on the beach at Wells-next-the-Sea following a winter snow shower a few days before Christmas in December 2009.

Winter is a great time to witness dramatic sunsets on the Norfolk Broads. In summer this view of Turf Fen drainage mill on the River Ant would usually be completely blocked by holiday boats. However in the winter months, with the tourists long gone, the Broads have a completely different feel about them.

Opposite: After a dull afternoon waiting for the light to break on the north Norfolk coast I was almost on my way home having not taken a single picture that day when suddenly a small break in the cloud on the horizon started to appear. I was able to capture a few quick shots of the stormy sunset with the small fishing boat *Emma Lynne* in the foreground on the completely deserted shingle beach at Cley.

A high tide is captured here at first light as the salt marshes at Thornham Creek start to flood on the north Norfolk coast. In the background the old coal shed is the only building that remains of a once bustling Thornham Harbour.

Every winter this area of Horsey beach is taken over by the seals as they come up on shore to give birth. There are now so many visitors arriving to witness the seal pups first hand that English Nature has had to introduce viewing areas so that the visitors do not disturb the seals. Here a young seal pup on the beach is photographed on a cold winter's day.

As beach huts go you can't really ask for a much finer location than at Wells-next-the-Sea, looking out over a fantastic sandy beach with dunes on one side and a pine woodland on the other. There is something strange about seeing the beach covered in snow and here the vibrant colours add some much-needed warmth to a bitter afternoon, with wind and snow showers coming in from the North Sea.

View across a snowy farmland at last light.

Opposite: The red brick Weybourne towermill was originally built in 1850 as a five-storey mill housing three pairs of stones to grind wheat. Here the mill is illuminated by stormy light following a light snow shower on the north Norfolk coast on a December afternoon.

Overleaf: Light snow on deserted sand dunes at Holkham on a bitterly cold December day.

Norwich cathedral has dominated the city skyline for over 900 years. At 315 feet the tower, also known as the lantern, is the second tallest in the whole of England with only Salisbury Cathedral being taller. Here I was lucky enough to capture some fresh snow and a bright blue sky on a cold December morning.

The magnificent cloisters at Norwich Cathedral looking out on to the fresh snow. These cloisters are the second largest in the country and provide a peaceful oasis in the heart of the busy city.

Highland Cattle with their thick coats appear to be enjoying the wintry conditions in the Norfolk countryside.

Opposite: Morning winter sun diffused by mist and fog alongside the River Thurne on the Norfolk Broads.

A solitary tree is silhouetted against a colourful sunset following heavy snowfall on the outskirts of Diss.

An abandoned bicycle that has clearly seen better days in the middle of snow-covered Halvergate Marshes on the Norfolk Broads.

Overleaf: Hardley drainage mill on the River Yare was built in 1874 and, after a long restoration project, new sails and a cap were finally added in 2009. Moorings and a visitor's centre were also built next to the mill which is accessible by walking along the Wherryman's Way footpath. One of the most distinctive things about the mill is the lean it has developed over the years. After a few previous unsuccessful attempts at photographing it I was finally rewarded with some good wintry weather following a cold snap late in 2009.

St Mary's church at East Somerton is an abandoned ruin with no roof. One of its remarkable features is this huge oak tree growing in the middle of the nave.

Left: St Benet's Abbey by the River Bure was once one of the wealthiest Benedictine monasteries in the country. St Benet's is also unique because it was the only monastery in Britain not to fall during the Dissolution. Here a double rainbow arches over the ruined gatehouse to the abbey which also houses a derelict drainage mill built into its walls around 1775.

Horsey drainage mill captured during passing showers on the Norfolk Broads. The present mill at Horsey was rebuilt in 1912 as a five-story red bricked tower mill. The mill continued to work until 1943 when it was struck by lightning. With help from the Norfolk Windmill Trust restoration work was completed in 1961.

Opposite: Today Horsey mill is open to the public and it's possible for visitors to climb to the top to enjoy fantastic views over Horsey Mere and the surrounding countryside.

A colourful winter sunrise captured from the Eels Foot Inn at Ormesby, north of Great Yarmouth.

St Ethelbert's church at Thurton captured during a heavy snow shower.

Overleaf: The colourful beach huts at Wells-next-the-Sea are reflected in a tidal pool surrounded by fallen snow.

First light illuminates the dunes at Horsey beach on a winter's morning with dark clouds overhead.

Opposite: Turf Fen drainage mill on the Norfolk Broads was built around 1875 to drain the Horning Marshes. Here the mill is captured against the backdrop of a colourful sunset reflecting in the River Ant on a February afternoon.

The remoteness of Berney Arms drainage mill has always appealed to me and with plenty of shots already captured during the day I was determined to capture the mill at dawn. After misty conditions were forecast I decided to head to a nearby vantage point at dawn. Here I set up my camera gear on the opposite side of the river and used a long lens to pick out the mill rising above the mist in the distance.

Left: Boats reflecting in Thurne Dyke following a dramatic sunset with Thurne windpump seen in the distance.

A spectacular winter hoar frost covers the reeds around Ormesby Broad at dawn.

Opposite: In freezing temperatures near the River Thurne, interesting ice patterns have formed on this part of the flooded marshland.

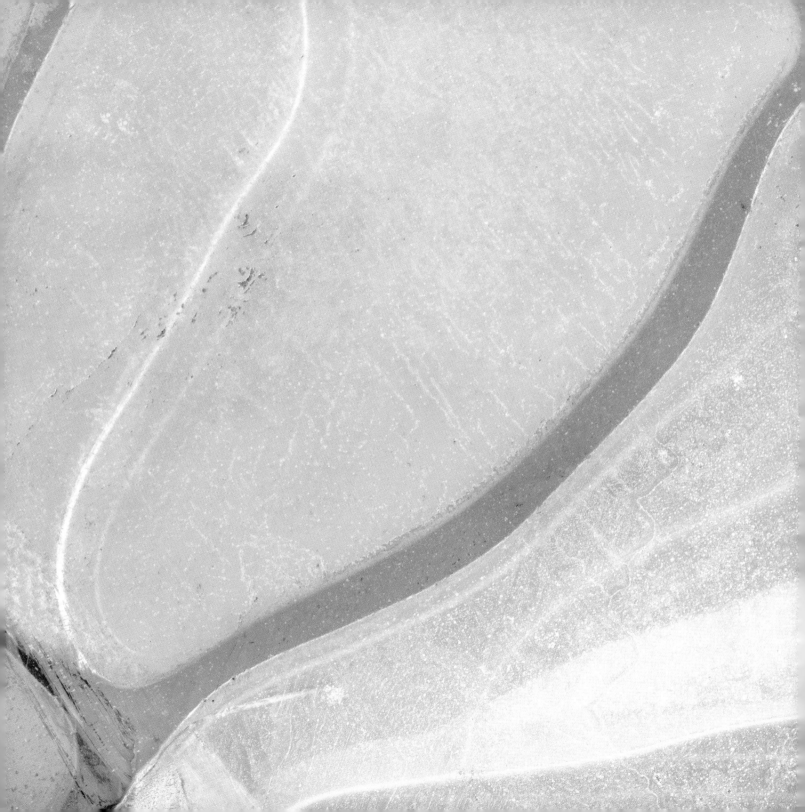

Reed has been harvested for centuries from the reed beds of the Broads and along the coast, providing valuable winter work for locals. Norfolk reed is famed for its quality and here the reeds are being cut in the traditional manner by a landowner on the Broads.

This scene was captured on a stormy afternoon at West Somerton, which has an excellent example of a traditional Norfolk round tower church. Round towers were built throughout East Anglia where the only real local stone to be found was flint. Most square towers required larger dressed stone for the corners before being covered in flint and mortar and for this reason square towers were considered more prestigious. Some round towers were later rebuilt in square form when the congregation could afford it.

Overleaf: A lone tree stands alone in the middle of a snow-covered field close to the village of Rollesby. In the distance, to the left of the tree, a yellow gritter lorry can be seen attending to the icy roads.

Christmas lights illuminate Holt Methodist church.

Opposite: Christmas lights and sculpture illuminated in the square on Haymarket in Norwich city centre.

Vibrant colours of a winter sunset light the sky behind Turf Fen drainage mill and are reflected in the mirror-like River Ant at How Hill. Winter is my favourite time to photograph this mill as the sun sets directly behind it at this time of year.

A fascinating art sculpture at Winterton-on-Sea, seen here brightly lit at first light on a cold winter's morning. The sculpture was made entirely from rubbish collected from the beach and reminds us what a variety of debris is washed up on to our coasts.

A traditional wooden sailing boat photographed on a tranquil misty morning on the River Thurne at dawn. The restored drainage mill of Thurne Dyke, which is owned and maintained by the Norfolk Windmills Trust, can be seen in the background.

Heavy winter snow covers Holt Woods. It snowed so much in such a short space of time that I struggled to drive out of the car park, almost having to dig myself out. However, just ten miles down the road they had no snow at all and it was completely dry.

Overleaf: The sun sets over a stretch of the River Waveney following light snow fall.

Snow patterns the deserted beach at Wells-next-the-Sea on the North Norfolk Coast. It always amazes me what a different feel this place has about it in the winter. In the summer it is packed with tourists and difficult even to park the car, but in the winter it is possible to have the entire beach to yourself.

I remember this particular afternoon at Turf Fen well. For most of the day the weather had been dull and grey, but about thirty minutes before sunset the clouds started to lift and I headed towards How Hill to shoot the sunset behind Turf Fen mill. But the usually short journey suddenly required a large detour after a tree had fallen down and was blocking the main road. Luckily after the detour I arrived just in the nick of time.

Low winter sun illuminates the leaning drainage mill at Hardley next to the River Yare on the Norfolk Broads.

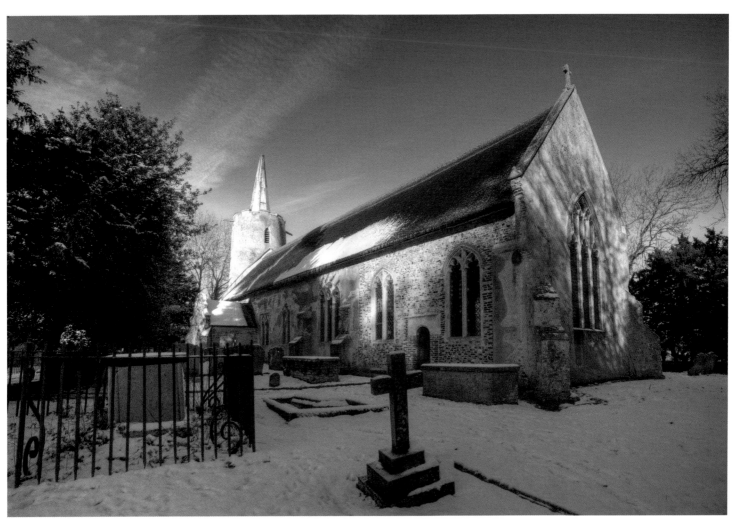

St Michael's Church at Stockton, north of Beccles, following a fresh winter snowfall.

St Peter Mancroft Church was built in the mid fifteenth century and is the largest of all the churches in Norwich. Situated between the Forum and the Market here the church is seen illuminated on a December night.

Norwich Guildhall was the centre of city government from the early fifteenth century until it was replaced by the present City Hall. The building contained various courts, a prison and a chapel. Here the building is decorated in festive Christmas lights.

The hulk of the shipwrecked *Sheraton* lies below the lighthouse at Old Hunstanton on the north Norfolk coast, captured here at sunset. Due to its position overlooking The Wash, Hunstanton is one of the few places on the Norfolk coast to witness the sun both rising and setting over the sea.

Opposite: A fine winter day captured here on the Halvergate Marshes close to Berney Arms windmill. At times it really does feel like this area of huge low-lying marshland is one of the most remote and exposed areas of the county.

Overleaf: Billingford windmill is located close to the town of Diss, just inside the Norfolk border. It is illuminated here by the warmth of the setting sun.

Tiny Hoveton church glows in the afternoon light following a short snow shower.

Delicate ice crystals cover the reeds in front of Thurne drainage mill on the Norfolk Broads.

Wind turbines on Blood Hill following a brief fall of snow. I regularly visit these spectacular structures for photography as they are just a short walk away from my house near Winterton.

A light dusting of snow at the picturesque West Somerton church. The thatched roof and the traditional round tower make this one of my favourite churches to photograph in the whole of Norfolk.

Overleaf: The massive Cantley sugar factory was originally built in 1912 and was the first such factory in the UK. Here the site was photographed on a December morning following a snowfall. When the factory is producing sugar a distinctive smell pervades the air over this part of Norfolk.

Ormesby Little Broad. This and Lily Broad are the two smallest of five broads that comprise the Trinity Broads, part of the National Park.

Left: A winter hoarfrost covers the reeds in front of this iconic Norfolk landmark. This image shows the remains of St Benet's Abbey gatehouse which later had a windmill built incongruously into the middle of it. The scene has been the inspiration for artists and photographers for well over a hundred years.

Left: Norwich City Hall illuminated by multicoloured lights as part of the Christmas decorations in the city centre.

Right & Opposite: Late night Christmas shopping in Norwich City Centre.

Holy Trinity church on a bright winter's morning following a light overnight snowfall in the small market town of Loddon.

The derelict sea defences on Happisburgh beach silhouetted against a wonderful winter sunrise on the Norfolk coast.

Despite being in a completely derelict state there is something quite beautiful about Brograve Level drainage mill. When I saw two walkers heading towards me I quickly selected a slow shutter speed to help blur the figures and add to the ghostly aspect of the ruin.

At most times of the day these posts next to the main car park at Thornham are completely dry, but when there is a high tide the posts, car park and surrounding marshland are completely flooded over by the incoming tide. Here with the help of some wellington boots I was able to capture the calm water at dawn.

Overleaf: The famous striped cliffs at Old Hunstanton are reflected in the wet sand at low tide on the north Norfolk coast.

Salhouse Broad at dawn on a winter morning on the Norfolk Broads.

Golden reeds are mirrored in the River Thurne on the Broads.

This has to be one of the most colourful sunrises I have ever witnessed. For around ten minutes the sky over Thurne drainage mill put on a fantastic display of colours changing from bright pinks to a fiery red before it completely faded about twenty minutes before sunrise, and then rain set in for the rest of the day.

Opposite: Ice crystals form in freezing fog, clinging to this spider's web captured on the Broads.

Norwich Castle standing high on an artificial mound is one of the region's most famous buildings. It was built by the Normans as a royal palace 900 years ago. The castle was used as a prison from the fourteenth century and later a museum in 1894. Here I visited Castle Meadow on a December evening to capture this picture of the castle illuminated at dusk.

Opposite: Norwich City Hall illuminated by a purple lights as part of the Christmas illuminations in the city centre.

Ormesby Broad on a winter's afternoon on the Broads.

Left: In my opinion the Norfolk Broads are at their most picturesque in the winter months when the reed turns a fantastic golden yellow colour. Here the reeds around the derelict Brograve level drainage mill are lit up by late sun on a stormy winter's afternoon at Waxham New Cut.

Overleaf: A light dusting of winter snow in the fields around Happisburgh lighthouse.

This view of a frozen Ormesby Broad was photographed on a February morning.

Opposite: A frosty morning at sunrise over Rollesby Broad.

Overleaf: One can almost feel the chill - a frozen field captured at dawn near Rollesby inleand from Caister.

86

Last of the Christmas shoppers browsing in shop windows on Fish Hill, Holt.

Christmas illuminations on Market Place in Holt town centre.

Overleaf: A spectacular winter hoarfrost covers the marshland around St Benet's Abbey. There was so much to photograph on this particular morning that I could have stayed out all day. However, after a couple of hours of walking through fields covered in frozen grass my toes were becoming so cold and painful that I couldn't wait to get home and get warm.

Golden winter reeds surround Ludham Womack Water drainage mill, seen here in the light of an early winter's morning.

A bright and clear sunrise over the Victorian pier at Cromer. It is said that a fishing pier or jetty has existed here since the fourteenth century, although the present structure dates only from 1901.

High tide captured at sunset on a winter's afternoon at Old Hunstanton on the north Norfolk coast.

Left: A robin bright against fresh snow in Thetford Forest.

A winter wonderland. A scene captured from the viewing platform high in the trees at Holt Country Park.

Opposite: The high tide leaves a wreck lying on the salt marshes at Thornham surrounded by sea water.

The Victorian Royal Arcade in Norwich was built and designed by Dereham-born architect George Skipper. The 247 foot arcade was finally opened in 1899. Today it contains a variety of shops, including the famous Colman's Mustard shop.

Christmas shoppers enjoying late night Christmas shopping in the Royal Arcade.

Overleaf: A pink dawn colours the frozen waters of Ormesby Little Broad.

Fantastic swirling patterns left from snow falling on to wet salt sand at Wells-next-the-Sea.

The last rays of the winter sunshine add warmth to this view of All Saints Church in Morston, standing against the backdrop of a blue sky following light winter snowfall.

Of all the places I regularly visit on the Norfolk coast Happisburgh is by far my favourite to photograph. It's a place that is constantly changing due to coastal erosion so no two visits are ever the same. It always amazes me how calm and quiet the sea can be here on some days compared to the often stormy North Sea conditions.

Hardley windpump was built by Ludham millwright Dan England in 1874. It was thought the mill continued to work draining the marshes until 1850 when it was badly damaged in a storm. In 1991 a group of volunteers came together came together to set about restoring the drainage mill and the sails and cap were finally returned to the mill in 2009.

Overleaf: A giant Christmas tree stands outside the Forum in Norwich City Centre.

The crowds have gone home and Chapelfield shopping centre lies quiet late on a December evening.

St Peter Mancroft Church and the forum illuminated at night. The clock tower of Norwich City Hall is seen in the distance.

The fifteenth century flint archway at Pulls Ferry marks the start of an ancient canal built by the monks to ferry stone for building Norwich Cathedral. Here Pulls Ferry is reflected in the waters of the River Wensum on a snowy Norwich morning.

Opposite: The newly restored Hardley drainage mill stands proud against the backdrop of a bright blue sky.

Overleaf: Turf Fen windpump and the River Ant at sunset on the Norfolk Broads. Unlike windmills which were built to grind corn, windpumps or drainage mills as they are also known, were used to drain the surrounding marshland.

Snow tops the gravestones in Bramerton churchyard

Opposite: High tide at Thornham creek, dawn.

A field of snow and, beyond, a twisted tree trunk adds drama to this wintery scene near Thurne.

Early morning light throws deep shadows across the derelict Brograve drainage mill on the Waxham New Cut.

St Ethelbert's Church on a winter's morning following a light overnight snow shower.

The low winter sun casts a wonderful warm glow on the red brick of St Benet's Level drainage mill beside the River Thurne on the Broads.

Opposite: The extensive dune system at Horsey are illuminated by the morning winter sunlight.

Overleaf: Frozen reeds swaying in the wind at Ormesby Broad at dawn on a winter's morning.

Low winter sun catches the incoming tide rolling over the zig-zag shaped groynes on Hunstanton beach.

Opposite: A dramatic winter hoarfrost coats a dead stem in delicate ice crystals – captured at first light in the Norfolk countryside.

Jarrolds department store, situated at the corner of Exchange Street and London Street, is a family run business in the heart of Norwich. It is perhaps the most famous store in the whole of Norfolk.

Jarrolds department store illuminated at Christmas in Norwich City Centre.

Christmas window display at Jarrolds department store.

Left: Jarrolds flagship store in the heart of Norwich was designed and built by Norfolk-based architect George Skipper who also designed the nearby Royal Arcade.

Overleaf: Fantastic pastel colours illuminate the sky above Cromer Pier at dawn on the Norfolk Coast.

A chill winter breeze gently stirs ice-coated reeds beside Breydon Water on the Norfolk Broads.

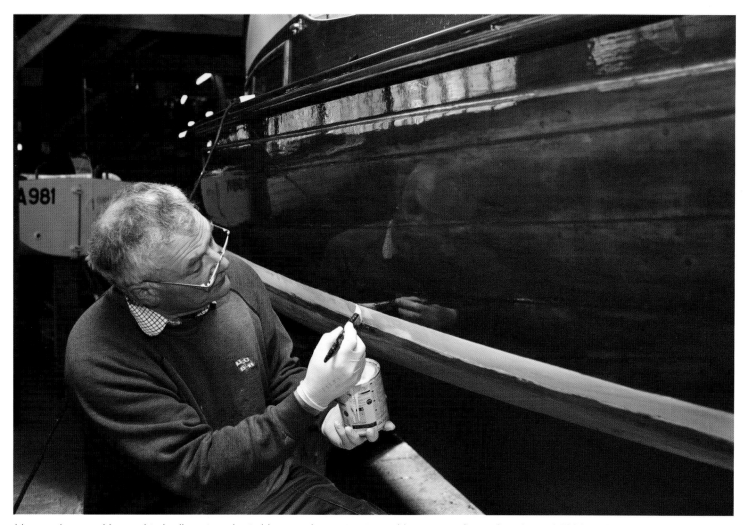

Hunters boatyard located in Ludham is a charitable trust that maintains and hires out a fleet of traditional 1930s sailing boats. In the winter months the boats are brought in for maintenance and a fresh coat of varnish.

Hustler undergoing repair work in the Hunters boatyard at Ludham. No vessels in the Hunters fleet have engines or electricity; instead hirers need to rely on wind power and oil lamps.

Overleaf: Lights from Cromer Pier reflect into the sea at dusk. On the end of pier is the famous Pavilion Theatre.

An intense sunset behind the white-painted structure of Thurne drainage mill at the head of Thurne Dyke on the Norfolk Broads.

Marshland beside the River Bure is transformed into a magical wonderland following an overnight hoarfrost on the Broads.

Overleaf: Threatening storm clouds pass overhead at Holkham bay on the north Norfolk coast. This fantastic beach is often completely deserted in the winter months and, for me, when the crowds have moved o, this is when it is at its best.

A March afternoon at Martham Staithe on the upper reaches of the River Thurne. Martham is a traditional and historic British village, the Saxons settled here about AD600 and gave the village it's name, 'the ham of the martens' – the home of the polecats. Living in the village myself, this particular stretch of the Norfolk Broads is right on my doorstep. This part of the River Thurne along with areas of Horsey, Hickling and West Somerton are some of the most peaceful and unspoilt areas of the entire Broadland region. Much of this is down to the very low bridge at Potter Heigham under which only smaller vessels can pass.